DENALI NATIONAL PARK
AN ALASKAN ECOSYSTEM

Creating Graphical Representations of Data

Kerri O'Donnell

Math
for the
REAL World™

Rosen Classroom Books & Materials™
New York

Published in 2006 by The Rosen Publishing Group, Inc.
29 East 21st Street, New York, NY 10010

Book Design: Haley Wilson

Photo Credits: Cover (background), pp. 3, 4, 8, 14 (title), 15 (taiga), 20, 24 (title), 30 (title), 31, 32 ©
Charles Mauzy/Corbis; cover (moose) © DigitalVision; p. 5 (map) © MAPS.com/Corbis; p. 5 (McKinley) ©
Steve Kaufman/Corbis; pp. 7, 14 (bears), 25 (willow ptarmigan) © Alissa Crandall/Corbis; p. 9 (Mount
Hood) © Craig Tuttle/Corbis; p. 9 (Mount Rainier) © Terry W. Eggers/Corbis; p. 9 (Mount St. Helens) ©
Buddy Mays/Corbis; pp. 15 (tundra), 16, 25 (gray wolf) © Darrell Gulin/Corbis; p. 21 © Kennan
Ward/Corbis; p. 24 (hoary marmot) © George D. Lepp/Corbis; p. 30 (tourists) © Paul A. Souders.

Library of Congress Cataloging-in-Publication Data

O'Donnell, Kerri, 1972-
  Denali National Park, an Alaskan ecosystem : creating graphical representations of data / Kerri O'Donnell.
      p. cm. — (Math for the real world)
  Includes index.
  ISBN 1-4042-3365-2 (library binding)
  ISBN 1-4042-6083-8 (pbk.)
  6-pack ISBN 1-4042-6084-6
  1. Ecology—Mathematics—Juvenile literature. 2. Ecology—Graphic methods—Juvenile literature. 3.
Denali National Park and Preserve (Alaska)—Juvenile literature. I. Title. II. Series.
  QH541.15.M34O36 2006
  001.4'226—dc22
                                        2005016485

Manufactured in the United States of America

CONTENTS

THE WONDER OF DENALI

Denali National Park in south-central Alaska is one of the world's most spectacular wildlife regions. Looking out across the park, you can see **taiga** and **tundra** stretching for miles before you. You can see rivers snaking through the landscape and mountainsides dotted with caribou and sheep. You might even see a gray wolf or grizzly bear searching for food.

Denali National Park is a place where the definition of the word "ecosystem" can be clearly understood. An ecosystem is made up of an area's physical and **biological** environments. The physical environment consists of the area's soil, water, air, and weather. The biological environment consists of all living things within the area. The relationships between these environments create an ecosystem.

Every moment, countless examples of the relationships within Denali's ecosystem can be seen. For example, blueberry bushes grow from the tundra soil. Small, mouselike animals called voles eat the blueberries. Wolves eat the voles. After the wolves die, their bodies are returned to the soil. All life is connected.

Denali National Park is the only national park in the world that contains a complete ecosystem within it. It has been called a "living tapestry." In this book, we'll find out more about Denali's fascinating ecosystem. We'll also learn how to create different graphs that display facts about Denali.

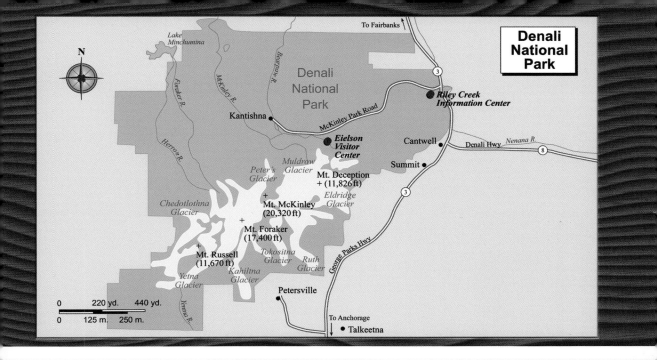

Denali National Park

Because it is the highest peak in North America, Mount McKinley is often called "the top of the continent."

In 1906, a hunter and **conservationist** named Charles Sheldon came to the Denali area to hunt Dall sheep, a species of North American wild sheep related to bighorn sheep. As he pursued the Dall sheep across Denali's landscape, he was astounded by the area's beauty. Sheldon fell in love with the region and returned the following year. He saw that large numbers of sheep were being killed by **commercial** hunters, and he worried that this would harm the balance of life within the area. He and other conservationists fought to preserve the area.

In response to these efforts, Congress established the area as a national park in 1917. It was first called Mount McKinley National Park. It was named after Mount McKinley, which is North America's highest peak. Mount McKinley is 20,320 feet (6,194 m) tall. Found in the southwestern part of Denali National Park, Mount McKinley is the park's main attraction. The mountain was named after William McKinley, the president of the United States from 1897 to 1901. Long before this, Native Americans of the area had named the mountain *Denali*, which means "The High One." Sheldon had always wanted to name the area Denali National Park. This finally occurred on December 2, 1980, when President Jimmy Carter signed a bill to rename the park Denali.

Here, a Dall sheep stands on a hillside with Mount McKinley in the background. Dall sheep live at high elevations near rocky terrain where they can escape from their enemies.

GRAPHING MOUNTAINS

Mount McKinley is part of the Alaska Range, which is a part of the Pacific Mountain System. Though it is North America's highest mountain, it is just 1 of many great peaks in mountain systems throughout North America. How does Mount McKinley's height compare with other mountains throughout North America?

As we've learned, Mount McKinley stands at a height of 20,320 feet (6,194 m). Mount Hood, found in the Cascade Range in Oregon, is 11,239 feet (3,426 m) high. Mount Rainier, found in the Cascade Range in Washington, is 14,410 feet (4,392 m) high. The Cascade Range's most active volcano, Mount St. Helens, is in Washington and stands 8,364 feet (2,549 m) high. In Mexico, a mountain called Pico de Orizaba stands at a height of 18,410 feet (5,611 m). The best-known mountain in the Rocky Mountains is Pikes Peak in Colorado. It stands at a height of 14,110 feet (4,301 m).

That might seem like a lot of information to keep straight when you read it in a paragraph like the one above. If we created a simple graph to show this information, however, it would be much easier to organize and compare the data. A graph can show us just how much taller Denali National Park's Mount McKinley is than the other mountains listed here.

Mount Hood, Mount Rainier, and Mount St. Helens are all in the Cascade Range, which extends south to California's Sierra Nevada and north to the Coast Mountains in British Columbia, Canada.

MOUNT HOOD

MOUNT RAINIER

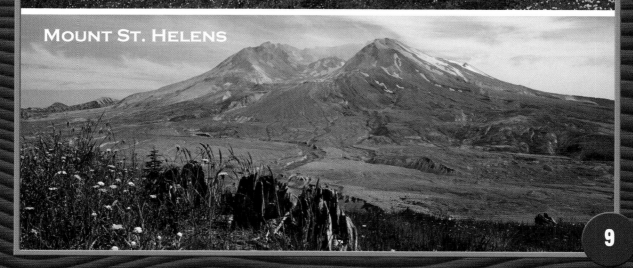

MOUNT ST. HELENS

A graph is a drawing that shows how quantities are related to each other. Graphs are used to convey information in a visual form so it is easier to understand.

To create a graph showing the heights of Mount McKinley and the other mountains on page 8, we first have to choose what kind of graph we want to use to represent the information. Let's take a look at some basic graphs.

A line graph uses points connected by a line to compare different values. It has both a horizontal **axis**—known as the x-axis—and a vertical axis—known as the y-axis. Line graphs are often used to show a change in value over a certain period of time. Let's look at a sample to understand how a line graph is constructed.

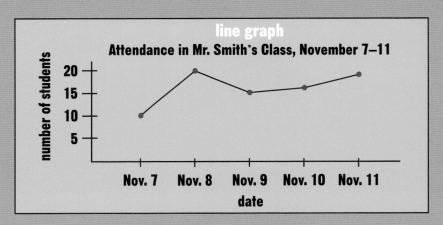

This line graph shows the number of students in class for each day of a particular week. The y-axis represents the number of students in class. The x-axis represents days of the week. By looking at all the information on the graph—the name of the graph, the labels along each axis, the values shown, and the line that connects those values—we can answer many questions about the class's attendance during that week and how it changed from day to day.

The same information shown in the line graph on page 10 can also be shown using a bar graph. A bar graph also has a y-axis and an x-axis, but uses bars of different lengths to express different values rather than using points connected by a line.

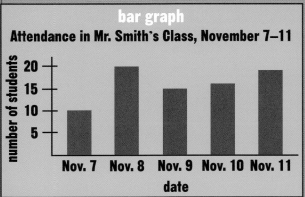

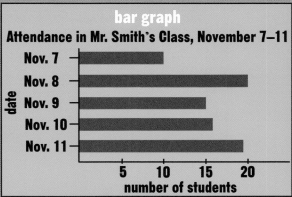

By comparing the line graph and the bar graphs, we see that although they are set up differently in some ways, they all communicate the same information. Even when we switch the y-axis and x-axis on the bar graph, the graph still tells us the same information.

Pie graphs—sometimes called circle graphs and pie charts—use different-sized "slices" to show how different values add up to a whole. For example, let's say that 20% of Mr. Smith's class chose soccer as their favorite sport, 50% chose football, and 30% chose baseball. We could use a pie graph to express that information.

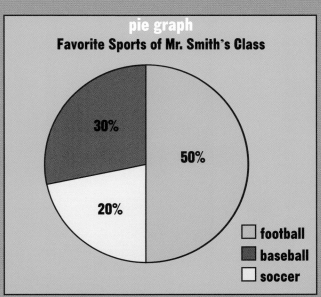

Let's use what we learned on page 8 about Mount McKinley and other North American peaks to make a simple bar graph comparing their heights. First, let's make a table to help us organize the information. We can organize the table by height, starting with the highest mountain, Mount McKinley.

mountain	height in feet
Mount McKinley	20,320
Pico de Orizaba	18,410
Mount Rainier	14,410
Pikes Peak	14,110
Mount Hood	11,239
Mount St. Helens	8,364

To show this information in the form of a bar graph, we first have to decide how to set up the y- and x-axes. Let's use the y-axis to show height in feet, labeled "height in feet," and the x-axis to show the different mountain names, labeled "mountain." We can then add the names of the mountains along the x-axis and choose a **scale** for the height measurement along the y-axis. For this graph, let's create a scale along the y-axis in **increments** of 1,000 feet.

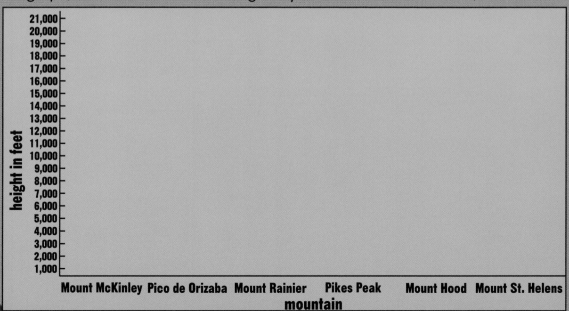

Using the numbers along the y-axis and the mountain names along the x-axis to guide you, mark where the top of each bar should be to represent each mountain's height. For instance, mark the spot over "Mount McKinley" on the x-axis that matches a height of 20,320 feet along the y-axis. Then mark the spot over "Pico de Orizaba" that matches a height of 18,410 feet, and so on. You'll need to estimate where the tops of the bars should be since you're using a scale with increments of 1,000 feet. When you have marked all the mountain heights on the graph, you can use a straightedge to draw in the bars.

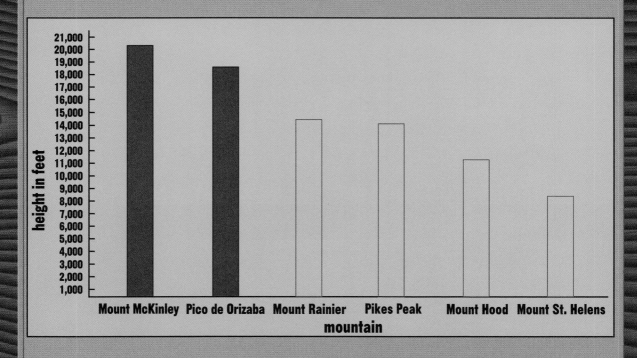

You can use your completed bar graph to answer questions about these 6 North American peaks. For example, which is the second-highest of these 6 peaks? Which is taller, Mount Rainier or Mount Hood? Which 2 mountains are the closest in height?

Taiga and Tundra

Only animals and plants that have adapted to long, freezing winters and brief growing seasons can survive in Denali. Denali National Park is made up of 2 **biomes**: taiga and tundra. The taiga covers the park's lower elevations. The taiga's growing season is short—about 100 days out of the year. White and black spruce are the most common trees found in the taiga, but they grow only to about $\frac{1}{4}$ the height of spruce trees that grow farther south. There are also quaking aspen, paper birch, and balsam poplar trees. Mosses and **lichens** grow on the forest floor, and shrubs such as blueberry bushes grow in the open areas.

As you travel farther north or higher into the mountains, the taiga turns into tundra. In the tundra, the cold temperatures, strong winds, and lack of moisture prevent trees from growing. Here, only short grasses, small shrubs, and tiny wildflowers can grow. In valleys between mountains, a mix of taiga and tundra plants and animals live together. Some animals hunt or feed in 1 area, then nest in another. Grizzly bears leave their tundra homes to hunt and might follow a moose into the taiga forest. A falcon makes its nest in the taiga forest but hunts above the tundra, looking for mice to feed on. Again, this demonstrates the complex relationships between the plants and animals of Denali's ecosystem.

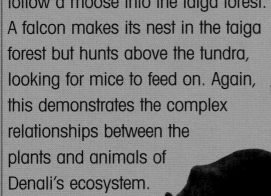

TAIGA

TUNDRA

Grizzly bears, like the mother grizzly and her cubs at left, generally live in Denali's treeless tundra, where they eat berries and grasses. They also eat fish from Denali's rivers and streams and hunt land animals like moose and caribou in the taiga.

The lack of trees in the tundra leaves it exposed to strong winds, and the short plants must be able to survive in the rocky soil. Some plants have hairy leaves, which help protect them from the cold wind. Some plants have waxy leaves to help hold in moisture, which is scarce in the tundra.

Like the taiga, Denali's tundra also has a very short growing season. Plants grow during the few months of the year when snow does not cover them and the temperatures are less harsh. Look at the table on page 17 to see the average high temperatures in Denali for the months of May through September, when most tundra plants grow.

Bearberries, which are high in protein, are an important part of the diet of grizzly bears and of some birds.

month	average high temp (°F)
May	59
June	70
July	72
August	66
September	54

We can create a line graph based on the information in the table above. First, draw your x-axis and y-axis. The x-axis can be labeled "month" and should include the 5 months on the table. Label the y-axis "average high temperature (°F)" and include a scale that corresponds to the information in the table. Let's use a scale of 0°F to 80°F with increments of 10°.

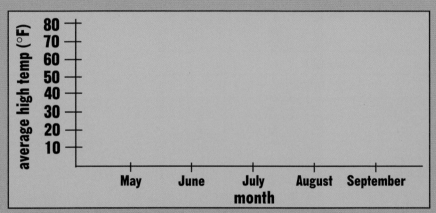

Now, plot the temperatures on the graph by putting a point at 59°F for May, 70°F for June, and so on. Then connect the points by drawing lines with a straightedge. You've made a line graph!

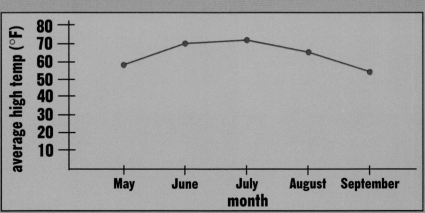

Your line graph shows average high temperatures in Denali from May through September. If you also had the average low temperatures for those months, you could use them to make a double line graph. A double line graph compares 2 sets of related data. In this case, the graph would show both Denali's average high and average low temperatures for May through September.

Below is a table showing Denali's average low temperatures for May through September.

month	average low temp (°F)
May	38
June	50
July	52
August	47
September	36

You can display this information on the graph you've already made by putting a point at 38°F for May, 50°F for June, and so on, as shown in the top graph on page 19. Then use a straightedge to connect the points, as shown in the bottom graph. By using a line that is a different color from the first line, you can show that the lines represent different sets of information. You need to add a key to identify the 2 lines. Notice that the y-axis is now labeled just "temp (°F)" because the graph displays data about average high *and* average low temperatures. Now your double line graph is complete.

You can use the graph to answer questions about Denali's high and low temperatures. Which month has the smallest difference between its average high and average low temperatures? What is the approximate difference between the graph's highest average high temperature and its lowest average low temperature?

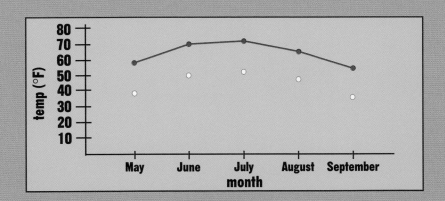

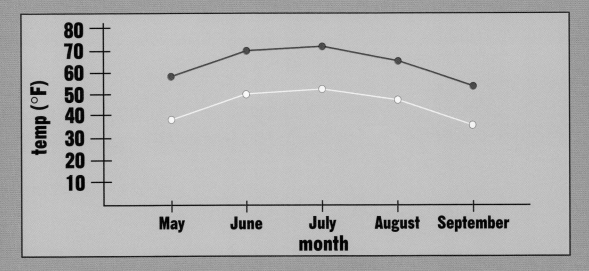

average high temperature (°F)

average low temperature (°F)

LAND OF DARKNESS AND LIGHT

Winter is Denali's longest season. Here, about 300 miles (483 km) south of the Arctic Circle, there is little sunlight during the long, cold winter months. This is because the North Pole is slanted away from the sun at this time of the year, and the northern areas of Earth receive less sunlight than they do during other times of the year. In the summer, the North Pole is slanted toward the sun, and Denali receives about 20 hours of sunlight a day. Plants do most of their growing during the summer months. Denali's animals are also affected by the dark winters and bright summers. When spring finally comes, bears that have been **hibernating** for many months wake up. Many of Denali's birds return after **migrating** to other places for the winter.

Animals also give birth to their young in the spring and spend the summer raising them. Mosquitoes and other insects return in the summer, and wild salmon fill Denali's rivers and streams. Grizzlies may eat 80 to 90 pounds (36 to 41 kg) of food per day during the summer and fall, fattening themselves up so they will be ready for their winter sleep. Young moose can gain up to 5 pounds (2.3 kg) a day, but only about 10% will survive their first year. Fall is the shortest season in Denali. The green tundra quickly turns fall colors, and the mating season begins.

Throughout the spring, summer, and fall, many of Denali's animals gather food to store so they can survive the winter, or to prepare for their next migration. It is an ongoing cycle.

These moose are grazing on summer grasses, preparing for the long, cold winter ahead. There are about 1,800 moose in Denali.

The table below shows Denali's average hours of daylight and darkness for May through September, when Denali's plants and animals are most active. We can use the information to create a double bar graph.

month	average hours of daylight	average hours of darkness
May	18	6
June	21	3
July	20	4
August	16	8
September	13	11

First, we draw our x-axis and y-axis. Label the x-axis "month" and include each of the 5 months on the table. Be sure to leave enough space between months on the x-axis to fit 2 bars for each month. Label the y-axis "hours" and include a scale that corresponds to the information in the table. Let's use a scale of 0 hours to 24 hours with increments of 1 hour.

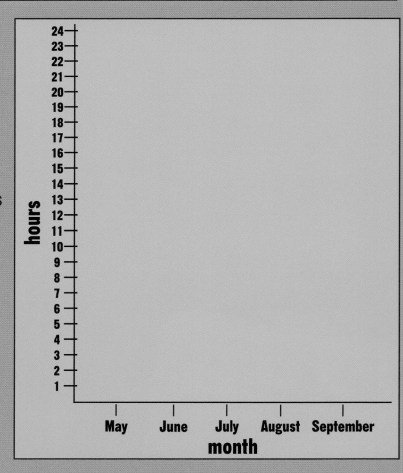

Using the numbers along the y-axis and the months along the x-axis to guide you, mark where the top of each bar should be to represent each month's average hours of darkness and daylight. For instance, over "May" on the x-axis, make a mark at 18 (for hours of daylight) and another mark next to it at 6 (for hours of darkness). When you have marked both sets of hours for all the months on the graph, you can use a straightedge to draw the bars. Be sure to include a key that shows which color represents hours of daylight and which color represents hours of darkness.

Now, color in each bar with the appropriate color as shown in the key. You've made a double bar graph!

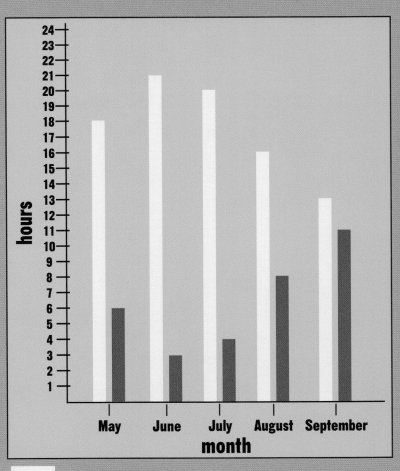

hours of daylight

hours of darkness

DENALI'S AMAZING ANIMALS

Some birds, like the chickadee, live year-round in Denali, remaining active during the winter months in order to survive. The chickadee weighs about $\frac{1}{2}$ ounce (14 g), but it will eat large amounts of stored seeds to maintain its weight so it can survive the winter. In 1 day, it can eat enough seeds to gain 10% of its body weight! This protects it from the cold.

The willow ptarmigan (TAHR-mih-guhn), Alaska's state bird, can maintain a body temperature of over 100°F (38°C) even when temperatures drop to almost –30°F (–34°C). The willow ptarmigan has feathers on its legs and feet to keep it warm. Its feathers change colors with the seasons.

Gray wolves roam the park all year long, hunting rodents, beavers, sheep, and even moose and caribou. A wolf may have a range covering between 25 and 150 square miles (65 and 389 sq km) and may travel up to 50 miles (80 km) a day in search of food.

Like grizzly bears, ground squirrels and **marmots** hibernate throughout the winter. During this time, their body functions almost stop so they can save their bodies' stored energy. Red squirrels and beavers spend the winter months tucked into their homes, eating whatever food they've managed to store during the warmer months.

HOARY MARMOT

WILLOW PTARMIGAN

GRAY WOLF

Denali's animals have adapted to their environment. As winter approaches, the ptarmigan molts its brown summer feathers and grows white feathers that help it blend into the snow. This allows it to hide from its enemies.

Denali is home to an estimated 39 species of mammals, 167 species of birds, and 10 species of fish. We can use this information to create a pie graph representing Denali's wildlife by animal group. First, let's make a table to organize the information.

animal group	number of species
birds	167
mammals	39
fish	10

When we add up the total number of species, we get 216 species. What portion of the pie graph will represent each group? As we learned on page 11, pie graphs use different-sized slices to show how different values add up to a whole. The pie graph we will create will have 3 slices, since 3 animal groups are being represented—birds, mammals, and fish.

Since a circle has 360°, the sections of the pie graph will add up to 360°. To find out how many degrees each section will be, divide the number of species in an animal group by the total number of species the pie graph will represent (216 species). Then, multiply that answer by 360°.

birds
$(167 \div 216) \times 360° = 278°$

mammals
$(39 \div 216) \times 360° = 65°$

fish
$(10 \div 216) \times 360° = 17°$

The answers above have been rounded to the nearest degree.
When we add the 3 rounded answers together, we get a total of 360°.

Now we can create our pie graph. You will need a compass and a **protractor**. First, use your compass to draw a circle. It will be easiest to measure the smallest section first, so start with the section representing fish, which will take up 17° of the circle. To do this, draw a straight line from the circle's center point to its edge. Then put your protractor on this **radius** and mark the point on the circle's edge that measures 17° from the radius. Use the protractor's straightedge to draw a line from the circle's center to the point you've marked on the circle's edge. This section shows Denali's fish species.

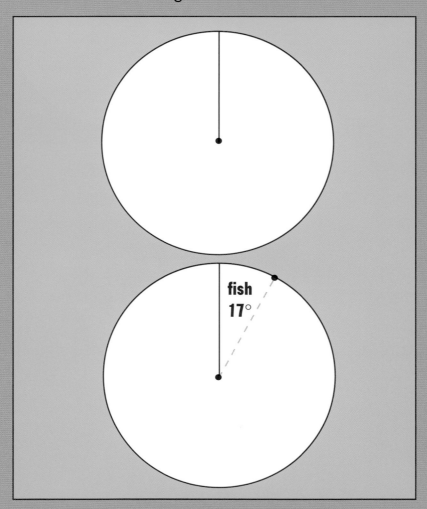

fish
17°

Now you can measure the next smallest animal group, the mammal group. To do this, use your protractor to measure 65° from the second line you drew on your graph and mark the circle's edge at that point. Use the protractor's straightedge to draw a line from the circle's center to the point you've marked on the circle's edge. This section of the pie graph represents Denali's mammal species.

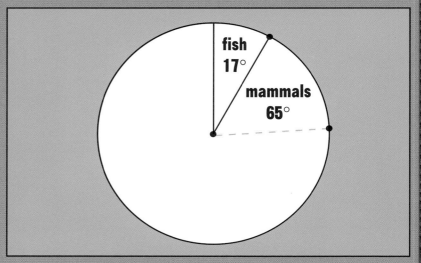

The third section of the graph will represent Denali's bird species. However, no more lines need to be drawn since the last slice of the pie graph represents the 167 species of birds at Denali, the park's largest animal group. Measure this slice to be sure that it is 278°. Now you can color each section a different shade. Don't forget to title your graph.

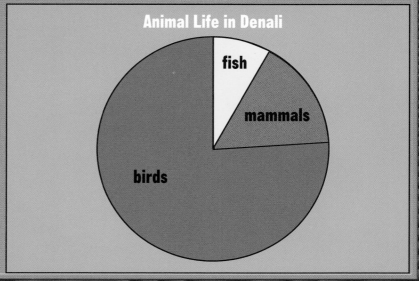

Animal Life in Denali

On page 22, we saw that Denali gets an average of 18 hours of daylight and 6 hours of darkness a day in May. Though we first used a double bar graph to show this, now we can follow the steps on pages 26–28 to show this information using a pie graph.

hours of daylight	hours of darkness
$(18 \div 24) \times 360° = 270°$	$(6 \div 24) \times 360° = 90°$

Use your compass to draw a circle. Measure the smallest section first, which will take up 90° of the circle. Draw a straight line from the circle's center point to its edge. Put your protractor on this radius and mark the point on the circle's edge that measures 90° from the radius. Use the protractor's straightedge to draw a line from the circle's center to the point you've marked on the circle's edge. This section of the pie graph represents Denali's average hours of darkness in May. The rest of the circle represents Denali's average hours of daylight in May. It should measure 270°. Label both sections and title your graph. Use different colors to shade each section.

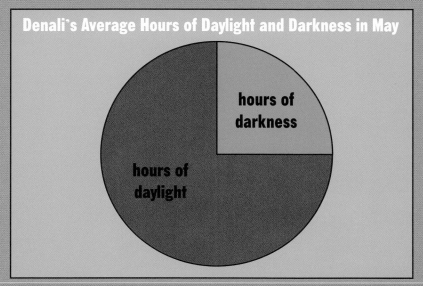

Denali's Average Hours of Daylight and Darkness in May

hours of darkness

hours of daylight

VISITING DENALI

People today can visit Denali National Park and see the vast wilderness of an ecosystem still largely untouched by human beings. Between 1923 and 1938, a 92-mile (148-km) road was built between McKinley Park Station and a mining camp to the southwest. This road made it easier for people to access the park, and the number of tourists who visit Denali each year has continued to increase. Hundreds of thousands of tourists visit the park each summer, traveling on tour buses that eliminate private car traffic in the park. This helps reduce the human impact on Denali, ensuring that people can enjoy the park for years to come without harming it.

We can study Denali to learn more about the complex and fragile relationships within its ecosystem. Knowing how to create graphs to convey the information we learn about its ecosystem can help us to understand these relationships even better and help protect this valuable national park in the future.

GLOSSARY

axis (AK-suhs) The main horizontal or vertical reference line of a graph.

biological (by-uh-LAH-juh-kuhl) Related to living things.

biome (BY-ohm) A major ecological community, such as a tundra, desert, or rain forest.

commercial (kuh-MUHR-shuhl) Related to trade or business.

conservationist (kahn-sur-VAY-shuh-nihst) Someone who wants to protect and preserve forests, rivers, and other natural resources.

hibernate (HY-buhr-nayt) To pass the winter in a state of deep sleep.

increment (IN-kruh-muhnt) One of a series of equal units added to a starting value.

lichen (LY-kehn) A living plantlike thing made of an alga and a fungus. Lichens grow on trees, rocks, and other surfaces.

marmot (MAR-muht) A burrowing squirrel-like animal with a short, bushy tail and very small ears.

migrate (MY-grayt) To move from 1 region to another when the seasons change.

protractor (proh-TRAK-tuhr) A tool shaped like a half circle that is used to draw or measure angles.

radius (RAY-dee-uhs) Any line from the center point of a circle to a point on its outside edge.

scale (SKAYL) A series of marks along a line with regular distances between them that are used to measure something.

taiga (TY-guh) A forest near the Arctic Circle that begins where the tundra ends.

tundra (TUHN-druh) A vast, treeless plain found in Arctic regions. The ground beneath the tundra's surface is always frozen.

INDEX